Shape Hunters

Shapes by the Sea

by Jenny Fretland VanVoorst

Bullfrog
Books

Ideas for Parents and Teachers

Bullfrog Books let children practice reading informational text at the earliest reading levels. Repetition, familiar words, and photo labels support early readers.

Before Reading

- Discuss the cover photo. What does it tell them?

- Look at the picture glossary together. Read and discuss the words.

Read the Book

- "Walk" through the book and look at the photos. Let the child ask questions. Point out the photo labels.

- Read the book to the child, or have him or her read independently.

After Reading

- Prompt the child to think more. Ask: Have you ever visited the seashore? What shapes did you see?

Bullfrog Books are published by Jump!
5357 Penn Avenue South
Minneapolis, MN 55419
www.jumplibrary.com

Library of Congress Cataloging-in-Publication Data

Fretland VanVoorst, Jenny, 1972– author.
 Shapes by the sea / by Jenny Fretland VanVoorst.
   pages cm.—(Shape hunters)
 "Bullfrog Books are published by Jump!."
 Summary: "Carefully leveled text and beautiful full-color photographs take beginning readers on trip to the seashore and encourages them to recognize shapes they see there."—Provided by publisher.
 Audience: Ages 5–8
 Audience: K to grade 3
 Includes index.
 ISBN 978-1-62031-202-5 (hardcover: alk. paper) —
 ISBN 978-1-62031-255-1 (paperback) —
 ISBN 978-1-62496-289-9 (ebook)
 1. Shapes—Juvenile literature.
 2. Seashore—Juvenile literature. I. Title.
 QA445.5.F745 2016
 516.15—dc23
                                    2014048980

Series Designer: Ellen Huber
Book Designer: Lindaanne Donohoe

Photo Credits: All photos by Shutterstock except: iStock, 6, 14–15; Thinkstock, cover, 5, 17, 22bl, 23bl, 23br.

Printed in the United States of America at Corporate Graphics in North Mankato, Minnesota.

Table of Contents

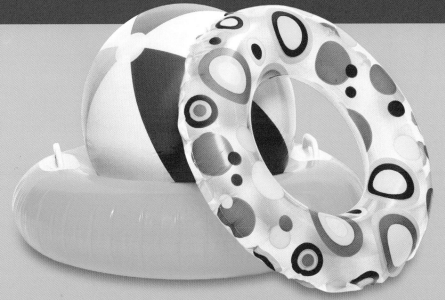

Sea Shapes

The seashore is full of shapes.

How many can you find?

Look at Mia's towel.
Look at its pattern.
Circles!

Dante makes
a sand castle.

8

He puts a flag on top.
It's a triangle.

The sand is wet.
Ann draws
a heart.

11

Let's swim!

The sign tells us it's safe.

What shape is it?

A rectangle.

Amal puts on his goggles.
See the ovals?

Now he can
see underwater.

Look at all the fish!

Look at all the circles!

Now he can
see underwater.

Look at all the fish!

Look at all the circles!

Dan spots a sea star.

Its shape is in its name.

Oh, no!
This triangle
means danger.
If you see this
shape, what
do you do?

More Shapes by the Sea

circle

stars

hearts

diamond

22

Picture Glossary

goggles
Special eyeglasses worn to protect the eyes from water or dust.

pattern
Colors and shapes that repeat in a certain order.

oval
A shape that looks like a circle that is narrower at the ends.

sea star
A sea animal that has a body shaped like a star.

Index

To Learn More

Learning more is as easy as 1, 2, 3.

1) Go to www.factsurfer.com

2) Enter "shapesbythesea" into the search box.

3) Click the "Surf" button to see a list of websites.

With factsurfer.com, finding more information is just a click away.